FOREVER

BY SAFI.S.S

Chapter 1: The Unseen Connection

Kyoto University buzzed with life. Students moved about in groups, laughter and conversation filling the air. The sprawling campus was a blend of modern architecture and traditional Japanese gardens, where students often gathered to study or relax. Among the bustling crowd was Haruto Kameda, the most popular guy in the university. With his charming smile, impeccable manners, and leadership in various clubs, Haruto was admired by everyone. Yet, beneath the surface, his heart was captivated by someone who didn't even realize it—Ayaka Nakamura.

Haruto's days were a whirlwind of activities—managing club events, studying, and effortlessly navigating social circles. On the surface, he appeared to be the perfect student, always surrounded by admirers and friends. His best friend Ryota often joked that Haruto could run for student president and win by a landslide. But for all his popularity, Haruto harbored a secret: a profound loneliness that came from the *pressure to always meet others' expectations. Beneath his confident exterior, he longed for a connection that was genuine and free of pretense.*

"Haruto, are you coming to the basketball game tonight?" Ryota asked, slinging an arm around his shoulder as they walked across the quad. "The team's counting on you to give one of your motivational speeches."

Haruto chuckled, adjusting his bag. "I'll try to make it. But I have a literature assignment to finish first."

"Classic Haruto," Ryota teased. "Always balancing ten things at once and still making time to be everyone's favorite guy."

Haruto smiled, but the comment stung more than he let on. Being "everyone's favorite guy" often meant hiding his true feelings. And lately, those feelings were centered on Ayaka Nakamura.

Ayaka was a simple and quiet girl. She wasn't the kind of person who stood out in a crowd. An average student with a love for reading and an affinity for helping others, she lived in her little bubble. Her favorite spot was a secluded bench under a cherry blossom tree, where she would spend hours lost in novels. Unassuming, she was the kind of person you might pass by without a second glance. But to Haruto, she was extraordinary.

Haruto had admired Ayaka from afar, drawn by her calm demeanor and the sincerity that radiated from her actions. He first noticed her during a campus cleanup event, where she worked quietly and diligently, helping an elderly janitor carry supplies. Her kindness left an impression on him. From that day, his eyes seemed to find her in every crowd.

Ayaka's world, however, was much smaller. She preferred the solace of the library to the noise of social gatherings. She often wondered if her invisibility was a blessing or a curse. Being unnoticed allowed her to avoid the pressure of standing out, but it also meant she rarely felt truly seen.

One evening, Ayaka found herself sitting by the campus pond, a book resting on her lap. The golden hues of the setting sun reflected on the water, creating a serene atmosphere. She closed her book and gazed at the ripples, her thoughts wandering. Did she belong here, among so many vibrant personalities? She sometimes felt like a background character in someone else's story.

Unbeknownst to her, Haruto passed by, his steps slowing as he noticed her by the pond. There was something captivating about the way she sat there, lost in thought. He wanted to approach her, to strike up a conversation, but he hesitated. What would he even say? Instead, he kept walking, his heart heavy with a longing he couldn't quite explain.

One day, during a lecture on Japanese literature, Haruto found himself stealing glances at Ayaka, who was scribbling notes with intense focus. The way she furrowed her brow when concentrating made him smile. He was so engrossed in watching her that he didn't notice Ryota leaning over.

"You've been unusually distracted, Haruto," Ryota whispered, a mischievous grin on his face. "Care to share what's on your mind?"

Haruto quickly shook his head, his cheeks tinged with embarrassment. "It's nothing. Just thinking about the project deadline."

"Right. And the project deadline happens to be sitting two rows ahead of us?" Ryota teased, nodding toward Ayaka's direction. Haruto's face turned a deeper shade of red.

After class, the group gathered in the campus's central plaza. Ryota, never one to let things slide, brought up Haruto's distraction again. "Alright, Haruto. Spill it. You've been acting weird lately."

Misaki and Daichi turned their attention to Haruto with curiosity.

"It's nothing," Haruto insisted, trying to deflect. "Just a lot on my plate right now."

"Come on, Haruto. You're always there for us. Let us be there for you," Misaki said with a warm smile. Haruto hesitated, unsure how

to articulate the feelings he barely
understood himself.

"Fine, keep your secrets," Ryota said with a
mock pout, making everyone laugh. But deep
down, Haruto knew he couldn't keep this
hidden forever.

Later that evening, Haruto found himself
wandering toward the library. He didn't
have a specific reason for being there, but a
part of him hoped he might catch a glimpse
of Ayaka. Sure enough, she was seated in her
usual spot, surrounded by a stack of books.
The soft glow of the desk lamp highlighted
her serene expression as she read. Haruto

lingered near the entrance, debating whether

to approach her.

"Just say hi," he muttered to himself. But the

thought of interrupting her made him

hesitate. After a few moments, he turned and

left, his heart both heavy and light at the

same time.

Chapter 2: A Helping Hand

The rain came down in steady sheets, transforming the quiet campus pathways into rivers of glistening reflections. Ayaka stood just inside the entrance of the library, clutching her bag and staring out at the relentless downpour. She had stayed late to finish a particularly enthralling novel, losing track of time. Now, she was stranded without an umbrella and unsure of what to do. Her mind churned with worries: if she stayed too long, the library would close, but running through the storm seemed equally daunting.

Her options were limited. She could wait, but there was no sign that the rain would let up anytime soon. She could run, but the idea of arriving home soaked to the bone wasn't appealing. Lost in her thoughts, she sighed softly, her breath fogging the glass door she leaned against. Inwardly, she cursed herself for not checking the weather forecast before leaving home.

Unbeknownst to her, Haruto Kameda was approaching the library from the opposite side of campus, holding a large black umbrella. His meeting with the student council had run late, but his thoughts weren't on the agenda they had discussed. They were on Ayaka. He'd noticed her earlier that day, tucked away in her favorite library corner, engrossed in a book. Her quiet focus was something he admired, but it also intrigued him. What kind of stories captured her attention so completely?

As he neared the library entrance, his steps slowed. Through the glass, he saw her standing there, alone, her figure framed by the pale glow of the overhead lights. She seemed lost in thought, her face carrying an expression of quiet determination mingled with uncertainty. Haruto hesitated, his grip tightening slightly on the umbrella handle. Should he approach her? Would she find it odd or intrusive?

"It's just an umbrella," he muttered to himself, shaking off his doubt. Taking a steadying breath, he opened the door and stepped inside.

"Need some help?"

The voice startled Ayaka, and she turned quickly. Standing there was Haruto, his black umbrella dripping faintly onto the tiled floor. His presence was almost surreal, as if he'd stepped straight out of one of the novels she loved so much. She blinked at him, momentarily speechless.

"I...I'll manage," Ayaka stammered, though her hesitance betrayed her words.

Haruto's lips curled into a gentle smile. "Come on. I'm headed the same way. Let's share."

Before she could protest further, he stepped closer and held the umbrella out so it covered both of them. Ayaka hesitated for a moment, her cheeks flushing slightly, before finally nodding. Together, they stepped out into the rain.

The walk was quiet at first, the rhythmic patter of rain filling the silence between them. Ayaka clutched her bag tightly, unsure of what to say. She was hyper-aware of how close they were under the umbrella, their shoulders almost brushing. Haruto, sensing her discomfort, decided to break the silence.

"Do you always stay this late at the library?" he asked casually.

Ayaka glanced up at him, surprised by the question. "Not always. I just... got caught up in a book," she admitted.

"What were you reading?"

She hesitated. "It's a novel about two people who meet by chance and change each other's lives."

Haruto chuckled softly. "Sounds like a good story. Maybe you can recommend it to me sometime."

Ayaka smiled faintly. "Maybe."

As they walked, Haruto shifted the umbrella slightly to ensure she stayed completely covered, even though it meant his shoulder was now exposed to the rain. Ayaka noticed and felt a pang of guilt.

"You're getting wet," she said quietly.

"It's just water," Haruto replied, brushing off her concern. "Besides, I can't leave someone stranded in the rain."

His words carried a warmth that Ayaka hadn't experienced in a long time. For the first time in what felt like forever, she felt truly seen and cared for. Haruto's calm demeanor and unwavering kindness eased her initial awkwardness, and she found herself relaxing slightly as they walked.

By the time they reached the intersection where their paths diverged, the rain had lightened to a drizzle. Ayaka turned to Haruto, clutching her bag nervously. Her thoughts swirled: How could she express her gratitude without sounding overly formal or awkward?

"Thank you," she said softly, her voice almost drowned out by the fading rain. "I... I didn't want to bother anyone."

"You're not a bother at all," Haruto said, his tone sincere. "If you ever need help again, don't hesitate to ask."

Ayaka nodded, watching as he turned and walked away, his umbrella swaying gently in the misty rain. She stood there for a moment longer, feeling a strange warmth despite the cold droplets clinging to her skin. For reasons she couldn't quite articulate, that brief walk left an imprint on her heart, one she carried with her as she made her way home.

Chapter 3: The Coincidences

Over the next few weeks, Ayaka began noticing a curious pattern. Whenever she found herself in a predicament, Haruto was there. The first time it happened was during a particularly hectic morning when her bag strap snapped as she was walking to class. She was already running late, and the sudden mishap left her flustered as books and notes scattered across the pathway. As she knelt down to gather her belongings, she saw a familiar pair of shoes approach.

"Here, let me help," Haruto said, crouching to pick up her scattered papers.

"You don't have to," Ayaka protested weakly, her cheeks flushing at the sudden attention.

"I insist," he replied, his tone leaving no room for argument. He deftly gathered her things and carried them all the way to the lecture hall. Their arrival together did not go unnoticed, as curious glances followed them into the classroom. Ayaka shrank slightly under the weight of the stares, but Haruto remained unfazed, giving her a reassuring smile before heading to his seat.

Later that day, Ayaka found herself reflecting on the incident. Why had Haruto gone out of his way to help her? She couldn't quite understand it, but a small part of her felt grateful—and maybe a little flattered.

Another time, Ayaka was stuck on a challenging group project. The team had reached a deadlock over a crucial decision, and tensions were running high. Haruto, who happened to overhear their discussion in the library, approached with a thoughtful suggestion.

"Have you considered breaking it into smaller tasks and assigning roles based on strengths?" he offered casually.

The team paused, his words sinking in. "That's... actually a great idea," one of her group members admitted. With Haruto's input, they quickly reorganized and made significant progress.

"Thank you, Haruto," Ayaka said as the group dispersed. "I don't know how you always manage to show up at the right time."

He shrugged with a smile. "Maybe it's fate."

Despite his casual demeanor, Haruto couldn't deny the truth in his words. He had been keeping an eye on Ayaka, drawn to her quiet strength and the way she carried herself with grace despite her shyness. There was something about her that made him want to be there whenever she needed support.

Ayaka, on the other hand, found herself growing increasingly curious about Haruto. Why would someone as popular and accomplished as him go out of his way to help her? She began to observe him more closely, watching how effortlessly he interacted with others. Yet, his attentiveness toward her felt different, almost deliberate.

One rainy afternoon, Ayaka's umbrella broke as she was leaving the library. The wind had turned it inside out, leaving her stranded under the awning. She was debating whether to make a dash for it when Haruto appeared, once again carrying his trusty black umbrella.

"This is becoming a habit," he said with a playful smile. "Shall we?"

Ayaka laughed softly, the sound surprising

even herself. "I'm starting to think you have

a sixth sense for rescuing people."

"Maybe I do," Haruto replied, holding the

umbrella over both of them as they walked.

Their steps fell into an easy rhythm, the

shared silence between them feeling oddly

comfortable.

One afternoon, as they worked together in

the library on a shared assignment, Ayaka

finally mustered the courage to ask, "Why

are you always helping me?"

Haruto looked up from his notes, surprised by her question. "Why not? You deserve help as much as anyone else."

His answer was simple, yet it carried a weight that Ayaka couldn't ignore. For the first time, she felt as though someone truly saw her—not just as another face in the crowd, but as a person worth noticing.

Their interactions didn't go unnoticed by others. Misaki and Ryota frequently teased Haruto about his "heroic rescues," while Sakura couldn't resist teasing Ayaka about her newfound "knight in shining armor."

"Do you think he likes you?" Sakura asked

one evening as they prepared dinner in their

shared apartment.

Ayaka nearly dropped the plate she was

holding. "What? No! He's just being kind."

"Uh-huh," Sakura replied, clearly

unconvinced. "And I'm the emperor of Japan."

Ayaka rolled her eyes, but Sakura's words

lingered in her mind longer than she cared to

admit. That night, as she lay in bed, she

found herself replaying her recent

encounters with Haruto. The way he smiled,

the way he always seemed to know exactly

what to say—it all felt too genuine to be mere coincidence.

For Haruto, these moments with Ayaka were becoming the highlight of his days. Each time he saw her smile or heard her soft laugh, it felt like a small victory. Though he had yet to confess his feelings, he couldn't deny that they were growing stronger with every passing day.

Chapter 4: The First Message

The annual university cultural festival was in full swing. The campus, usually calm and studious, had transformed into a vibrant hub of activity. Colorful banners and stalls lined the pathways, and the air buzzed with laughter and chatter. Amid the festivities, Ayaka found herself assigned to a stall promoting the literature club, where she spent her day recommending books and discussing her favorite genres with visitors.

Haruto, as usual, was at the center of attention. He had been tasked with overseeing several events, and his charisma drew crowds wherever he went. Ayaka occasionally caught glimpses of him in the distance, his confident demeanor a stark contrast to her quiet nature.

Toward the end of the day, an announcement was made for all club members to exchange contact information to coordinate clean-up efforts. Ayaka hesitated as her phone was passed around, but eventually, she added Haruto's number to her contacts. The thought of having a direct line to him made her heart race, though she quickly dismissed it as a silly reaction.

Later that evening, Ayaka sat by her desk, staring at her phone. She debated whether to send a message to Haruto. What would she even say? Would it seem too forward? She sighed, placing her phone down, only to pick it up again moments later. After what felt like an eternity of hesitation, she typed out a simple message:

Ayaka: "Thank you for always helping me. I don't know what I would do without your kindness."

Her finger hovered over the send button before she finally tapped it. Immediately, doubt flooded her mind. What if he thought she was being too formal? What if he didn't reply at all?

Her phone buzzed almost instantly.

Haruta "You're welcome. I'm glad I could help. Let me know if you ever need anything."

Ayaka's lips curled into a small smile. His reply was warm, reassuring, and exactly what she needed to hear. That one message sparked a series of conversations that grew increasingly frequent over the days. At first, their exchanges were about mundane topics—assignments, events, and casual observations. But as they continued to text, their messages became more personal.

Haruto discovered Ayaka's love for classic literature and her dream of becoming a writer. In turn, Ayaka learned about Haruto's passion for leadership and his struggle to balance expectations with his own aspirations. These late-night conversations became the highlight of their days, though neither would admit it aloud.

One evening, Ayaka found herself opening up about her insecurities. "Sometimes I feel like

I'm just... invisible," she wrote, hesitant yet relieved to share something so personal.

Haruto's response was immediate and heartfelt. "You're not invisible to me. You're remarkable, Ayaka. More than you realize."

Ayaka stared at the screen, her chest tightening with an unfamiliar warmth. She reread his words several times, each repetition making her heart flutter.

Meanwhile, Haruto found himself waiting eagerly for Ayaka's messages. Her honesty and thoughtfulness were a refreshing change from the surface-level interactions he was used to. For the first time, he felt like someone truly understood him.

Their growing connection didn't go unnoticed by those around them. Misaki and Ryota often teased Haruto about his "constant texting," while Sakura playfully interrogated Ayaka about the identity of her mysterious late-night correspondent.

"So, who's the lucky guy?" Sakura asked one evening, leaning against the doorframe of their shared room.

"It's not like that," Ayaka insisted, her cheeks turning crimson.

"Uh-huh," Sakura said with a grin. "Just a friend, right?"

Ayaka nodded, though her heart told her otherwise.

The festival cleanup provided another opportunity for them to interact in person. Haruto found Ayaka struggling to carry a stack of heavy boxes from one stall to another.

"Here, let me take those," Haruto offered, relieving her of the load.

"You don't have to keep rescuing me, you know," Ayaka said, her voice tinged with embarrassment but softened by gratitude.

"Who says I mind?" Haruto replied with a playful grin. "Besides, it's not fair to let you do all the heavy lifting."

As they worked together to clean up, Haruto couldn't help but admire Ayaka's quiet determination. She didn't complain, even when the tasks were tedious, and she had a way of focusing on the little things that others overlooked. Watching her, Haruto felt an even stronger pull toward her.

When the cleanup was done, Haruto walked Ayaka back to her dorm. The night air was crisp, and the faint sound of distant music lingered in the background. They talked about their favorite parts of the festival, their laughter echoing in the quiet streets.

"Thank you for today," Ayaka said as they reached the entrance. "And... for everything else. I really mean it."

Haruto smiled, his gaze soft. "You don't have to thank me, Ayaka. I'm just glad I could help."

After they parted ways, Ayaka couldn't stop thinking about how effortless it felt to talk to Haruto. For someone who had always kept people at arm's length, letting him in felt surprisingly natural.

Meanwhile, Haruto found himself replaying their conversations in his mind, his heart lighter than it had been in a long time. For both of them, these moments marked the beginning of something they couldn't yet name but already cherished deeply.

Chapter 5: The Confession

Spring had arrived, painting Kyoto University in shades of soft pink as cherry blossoms bloomed across the campus. The air was filled with the scent of new beginnings, but for Haruto, the season carried a mix of anticipation and unease. His feelings for Ayaka had grown too strong to ignore, and he knew he couldn't let the academic year end without telling her how he felt.

Ayaka, unaware of Haruto's internal struggle, had been spending her days

immersed in preparations for final exams.
Despite her quiet nature, she had grown
more confident, thanks in part to Haruto's
unwavering support. Their late-night
conversations had become a constant in her
life, and she found herself looking forward to
his messages more than she cared to admit.

One afternoon, Haruto found Ayaka sitting
under a cherry blossom tree, her nose buried
in a book. The scene was so serene that it
made his heart ache. Clutching a small box
in his hand, he took a deep breath and
approached her.

"Ayaka," he called softly.

Startled, she looked up, her eyes widening as she saw him. "Oh, Haruto. Hi. What brings you here?"

Haruto hesitated for a moment before sitting down beside her. The soft petals fell around them, creating a picturesque backdrop that felt almost too perfect.

"I needed to talk to you," he said, his voice steady but his heart racing.

Ayaka closed her book, sensing the seriousness in his tone. "Is everything okay?"

He nodded, though his expression betrayed his nerves. "There's something I've been meaning to tell you for a while now."

She tilted her head, curiosity evident in her eyes. "What is it?"

Haruto took a deep breath, his fingers tightening around the box. "Ayaka... I've liked you for a long time. I don't know when it started, but every time I see you, I feel... happy. You've become an important part of my life, and I can't imagine not telling you how I feel."

Ayaka's lips parted in surprise, her cheeks turning a deep shade of pink. She opened her mouth to respond but hesitated, her gaze dropping to her hands.

"I... I'm sorry, Haruto," she whispered. "I can't."

Haruto felt his heart sink, but he forced himself to remain calm. "Why?" he asked gently. "If it's something I've done—"

"No," Ayaka interrupted, her voice trembling. "It's not you. It's me."

Her words only deepened his confusion.

"Then please, tell me. I want to understand."

After a long silence, Ayaka finally looked up, tears brimming in her eyes. "I have stage 2 blood cancer. I didn't want to tell anyone because... because I didn't want to burden them. If I... If something happens to me, I don't want you to suffer."

Haruto stared at her, his mind reeling. He hadn't expected this—not in a million years. But as the weight of her words settled, his resolve only grew stronger.

"Ayaka," he said firmly, taking her hands in his. "I don't care about that. I care about you. Let me be by your side, no matter what happens."

She shook her head, tears streaming down her face. "You don't understand. If we... if we get closer and then I... I don't want you to go through that pain."

"Do you think I'd be any less hurt if I stayed away?" Haruto countered, his voice breaking. "I'd rather have a little time with you than none at all. Please, Ayaka. Let me be there for you."

Their argument continued for what felt like hours, Ayaka's fear clashing with Haruto's determination. Finally, exhausted and overwhelmed, she nodded.

"Okay," she whispered. "But promise me one thing."

"Anything," Haruto said without hesitation.

"Promise me you'll never regret this."

Haruto smiled, his eyes glistening with unshed tears. "I could never regret loving you."

The days following Haruto's confession were not without challenges. Ayaka insisted on telling their families about her condition. Haruto's parents were initially apprehensive, their concern for their son evident in their worried expressions.

However, after meeting Ayaka and witnessing the bond between them, their fears began to fade.

"You have our blessing," Haruto's mother said one evening, taking Ayaka's hand in hers. "As long as you promise to lean on us when things get tough."

Ayaka's parents, though hesitant, also came to support their daughter's decision. Her father, a man of few words, sat Haruto down for a heartfelt conversation.

"Take care of her," he said simply. "She's been through so much already."

"I will," Haruto promised, his voice firm. "Always."

Haruto's friends, too, noticed the shift in his demeanor. Misaki and Ryota, always playful, couldn't resist teasing him about the way he lit up whenever Ayaka's name came up in conversation.

"Haruto, you're like a lovesick puppy," Ryota teased one afternoon. "You've got it bad, huh?"

Haruto laughed but didn't deny it. "Maybe I do," he admitted, his smile growing softer. "But I wouldn't change it for the world."

As for Ayaka, her own circle of friends rallied around her. Sakura, her roommate, became her biggest cheerleader, encouraging her to embrace the happiness Haruto brought into her life.

"You deserve this, Ayaka," Sakura said one evening as they shared a pot of tea. "Don't let fear hold you back."

Their support, combined with Haruto's unwavering presence, gave Ayaka the *courage to hope for a future she had once*

thought impossible. For the first time in

years, she began to envision a life filled with

love and joy—a life shared with Haruto.

Chapter 6: Love and Sacrifice

The days after Haruto and Ayaka became a couple were filled with moments of joy and trials that tested their resolve. Their friends, Misaki and Ryota, quickly embraced Ayaka as one of their own, often planning outings to take her mind off her treatments. Misaki, in particular, became a confidante for Ayaka, offering support and a listening ear when the weight of her illness felt overwhelming.

"You're not alone in this," Misaki reminded her one evening as they sipped tea at a cozy café. "We're all here for you."

Haruto's dedication to Ayaka never wavered. He accompanied her to every doctor's appointment, holding her hand during the grueling chemotherapy sessions. On days when the side effects left her too weak to get out of bed, he would sit by her side, reading her favorite books aloud or simply being there in silence.

Their friends often marveled at the depth of Haruto's devotion. "You're like a real-life knight in shining armor," Ryota joked one evening as they gathered for dinner.

"It's not about being a knight," Haruto replied with a small smile. "It's about being there for someone you love."

Despite the challenges, there were moments of lightness and laughter. Ayaka and Haruto found joy in the little things—trying new recipes, exploring the city's hidden gems, and spending lazy afternoons watching old movies. Their bond grew stronger with each passing day, their love a beacon of hope amid the uncertainty.

Two years later, the couple celebrated their wedding in an intimate ceremony surrounded by friends and family. The day was filled with laughter and tears, a testament to the love they had built despite the challenges they faced. Ayaka's father, who had been initially hesitant about the relationship, gave a heartfelt speech, thanking Haruto for bringing joy to his daughter's life.

"You've given her hope," he said, his voice trembling. "And for that, I will always be grateful."

The ceremony was simple but meaningful, held under a canopy of cherry blossoms. Misaki served as Ayaka's maid of honor, while Ryota proudly stood by Haruto as his best man. The vows they exchanged were heartfelt, reflecting the depth of their commitment to one another.

"I promise to love you in every season of life," Haruto said, his voice steady despite the emotion in his eyes. "Through every trial, every joy, and every moment in between."

"And I promise to trust in us," Ayaka replied, her voice trembling. "Even when I'm scared, I'll hold on to the love you've given me."

As they kissed, the cherry blossoms swirled around them, a symbol of their fleeting yet beautiful journey together.

Married life brought its own set of challenges, but Haruto and Ayaka faced them together. They found solace in each other's company, creating a home filled with love and understanding. Decorating their small apartment became a source of joy, with Haruto teasing Ayaka about her tendency to overthink every decision.

"Do we really need five different shades of blue for the curtains?" he joked, earning a playful glare from Ayaka.

"Yes," she replied firmly. "It's important to get it right."

Their days were a blend of ordinary routines and extraordinary love. Haruto's presence made even the most mundane tasks—like grocery shopping or folding laundry—feel special. And though Ayaka's treatments continued, she found strength in their shared moments of laughter and support.

But their bliss was not to last. One fateful afternoon, Ayaka collapsed at home. Panic gripped Haruto as he rushed her to the hospital, where doctors delivered grim news: her cancer had progressed, and she required a bone marrow transplant immediately. The odds of finding a match were slim, and time was running out.

Without hesitation, Haruto volunteered to be tested. When the results came back as a perfect match, relief flooded Ayaka's heart—but it was short-lived.

"There are significant risks involved," the doctor explained, addressing Haruto. "While the procedure is life-saving for the recipient,

there is a chance of severe complications for

the donor."

Ayaka's eyes filled with tears as she gripped

Haruto's arm. "No, Haruto. You can't. It's too

dangerous."

Haruto turned to her, his expression

resolute. "I'm not losing you, Ayaka. I'll take

the risk."

Despite her protests, Haruto signed the

consent forms, determined to save the

woman he loved. The night before the

surgery, they sat together in her hospital

room, the weight of unspoken fears hanging in the air.

"Promise me something," Ayaka said, her voice barely above a whisper.

Haruto reached for her hand. "Anything."

"Promise me you'll take care of yourself," she said, tears streaming down her cheeks. "If something happens, I..."

"Nothing's going to happen," he interrupted gently, pulling her into an embrace. "We're going to get through this together."

The surgery was a success for Ayaka, but complications arose for Haruto. His condition deteriorated rapidly, and despite the medical team's best efforts, he passed away the following day.

When Ayaka woke from her recovery, she was greeted with the news of Haruto's sacrifice. Her world shattered as grief consumed her. The man who had given her everything—his love, his strength, and ultimately his life—was gone.

For weeks, Ayaka struggled to find meaning in a world without Haruto. Their small apartment, once filled with laughter and warmth, felt unbearably empty. She clung to the memories they had created—the way he would hum softly while cooking, the gentle way he held her hand during her weakest moments, and the unwavering determination in his eyes when he promised to stay by her side.

Ayaka found solace in the letters Haruto had written to her before the surgery. In one of them, he wrote:

"I don't regret a single moment we spent together. Loving you has been the greatest honor of my life. If my sacrifice means you get to live, then I leave this world knowing I

did something right. Keep smiling, Ayaka.
You have a strength that inspires everyone
around you. Never forget that."

Those words became her anchor as she
navigated her grief. She returned to writing,
pouring her pain and love into stories that
touched the hearts of others. Her first novel,
dedicated to Haruto, became a symbol of
their love—a story of hope and resilience in
the face of loss.

Years later, Ayaka often visited the hill
where they had exchanged their vows. Under
the cherry blossom tree, she would sit with a
notebook in hand, writing letters to Haruto.

Though he was gone, his love remained a guiding force in her life, a reminder that true love transcends even the greatest of losses.

Chapter 7: Eternal Love

The seasons changed, and Ayaka's life entered a new chapter beyond the university, but for her, the world felt irrevocably altered. Haruto's absence was a void that nothing could fill. The man who had given her his heart—and ultimately, his life—was gone, but his memory lingered in every corner of her existence.

In the weeks following Haruto's death, Ayaka struggled to navigate the waves of grief that consumed her. She often found herself sitting beneath the cherry blossom tree where he had confessed his love, the place that had become a symbol of their bond. She would close her eyes and imagine him there, his warm smile reassuring her that everything would be okay.

For a time, it seemed impossible to move forward. The weight of guilt and sorrow threatened to crush her, but slowly, the love Haruto had given her began to guide her steps. She remembered his words, his unwavering belief in her strength, and she resolved to honor his sacrifice by living the life he had fought so hard to save.

One evening, while organizing their small apartment, Ayaka stumbled upon a drawer she hadn't opened in months. Inside, she found an envelope with her name written on it in Haruto's familiar handwriting. Her hands trembled as she picked it up, her heart pounding in her chest.

She sat down on their couch, tears streaming down her cheeks before she even opened the envelope. Taking a deep breath, she unfolded the letter and began to read.

"My Dearest Ayaka,

If you're reading this, it means I'm no longer by your side. I wish I could have stayed with you longer, to share more laughter, more quiet moments, and more love. But if this is the price I had to pay to ensure your smile, I pay it willingly.

Loving you has been the greatest gift of my life. Your kindness, your strength, and your beautiful soul have touched me in ways I never thought possible. You've taught me what it means to truly live.

I know the days ahead will be hard, and there will be moments when the weight of my absence feels unbearable. In those moments, remember this: you are never alone. My love will always be with you, in every cherry blossom that falls, in every warm breeze that brushes your face, and in every beat of your heart.

Live your life fully, Ayaka. Chase your dreams, embrace the world, and never stop smiling. You have a light within you that the world needs to see.

Thank you for loving me and allowing me to love you in return. You've made my life complete.

Forever yours, Haruto"

Ayaka clutched the letter to her chest, her sobs filling the silent apartment. Yet, amidst the pain, there was a sense of comfort—a reminder that Haruto's love would always be a part of her. She resolved to honor his words, to live a life that celebrated the love they had shared.

After graduating, Ayaka immersed herself in her writing, finding solace in the stories she crafted. Her pain poured onto the pages, transforming into tales of love, loss, and resilience. Encouraged by the memory of Haruto and the lessons he had taught her, she sent her first collection of stories to a local publisher. To her surprise and joy, it was accepted, marking the beginning of a promising literary career and a new chapter in her life.

Despite her growing success, Ayaka's heart remained tethered to Haruto. She often visited his family, sharing memories and *finding comfort in their shared love for him.*

Haruto's mother would hold Ayaka's hands and tell her, "You were the greatest joy in his life. Thank you for loving him as deeply as he loved you."

Ayaka also found herself drawn to volunteer work, inspired by Haruto's selflessness. She began spending her weekends at a local hospital, offering support to patients undergoing cancer treatment. Her presence became a source of comfort for many, her quiet strength and understanding resonating with those she helped.

One spring afternoon, Ayaka stood beneath the cherry blossom tree once more. The petals danced in the breeze, their soft pink hues a reminder of the fleeting beauty of life. She held a notebook in her hands, its pages filled with a story she had written—a story about a boy and a girl who had found love in the face of impossible odds.

She knelt by the tree and placed the notebook at its base. "This is for you, Haruto," she whispered, her voice trembling. "Thank you for teaching me how to love and for giving me the courage to keep going. I'll carry you with me, always."

As she stood, a single petal drifted down, landing on her open palm. Ayaka smiled through her tears, taking it as a sign that Haruto was still with her, watching over her as he had always promised.

Years passed, but Ayaka's love for Haruto never wavered. She went on to achieve great success as a writer, her stories touching countless hearts. Yet, no matter how far life took her, she always returned to the cherry blossom tree, the place where their love had blossomed and endured.

Though Haruto was gone, his love remained—a beacon of light that guided

Ayaka through her darkest days. In the whispers of the wind and the gentle rustle of petals, she felt his presence, a reminder that their bond was unbreakable.

Under the tree, Ayaka would often whisper, "I love you, Haruto. Forever."

And in her heart, she knew he was saying it back.

THE END

www.ingramcontent.com/pod-product-compliance
Lightning Source LLC
Chambersburg PA
CBHW020501160726
47991CB00007B/2766